Benjamin Boo
Plays Hide-and-Seek With You

DAWN BEHRENS

Four Petals Books

Published by Four Petals Books 2012

ISBN-10: 0985750022
ISBN-13: 978-0-9857500-2-2

The Benjamin Boo stories are dedicated
to my grandchildren, Madison, Andy, and Tristan.
Grandawn loves you very much!

Thank you to the readers who share my stories with your little ones. I feel very honored.

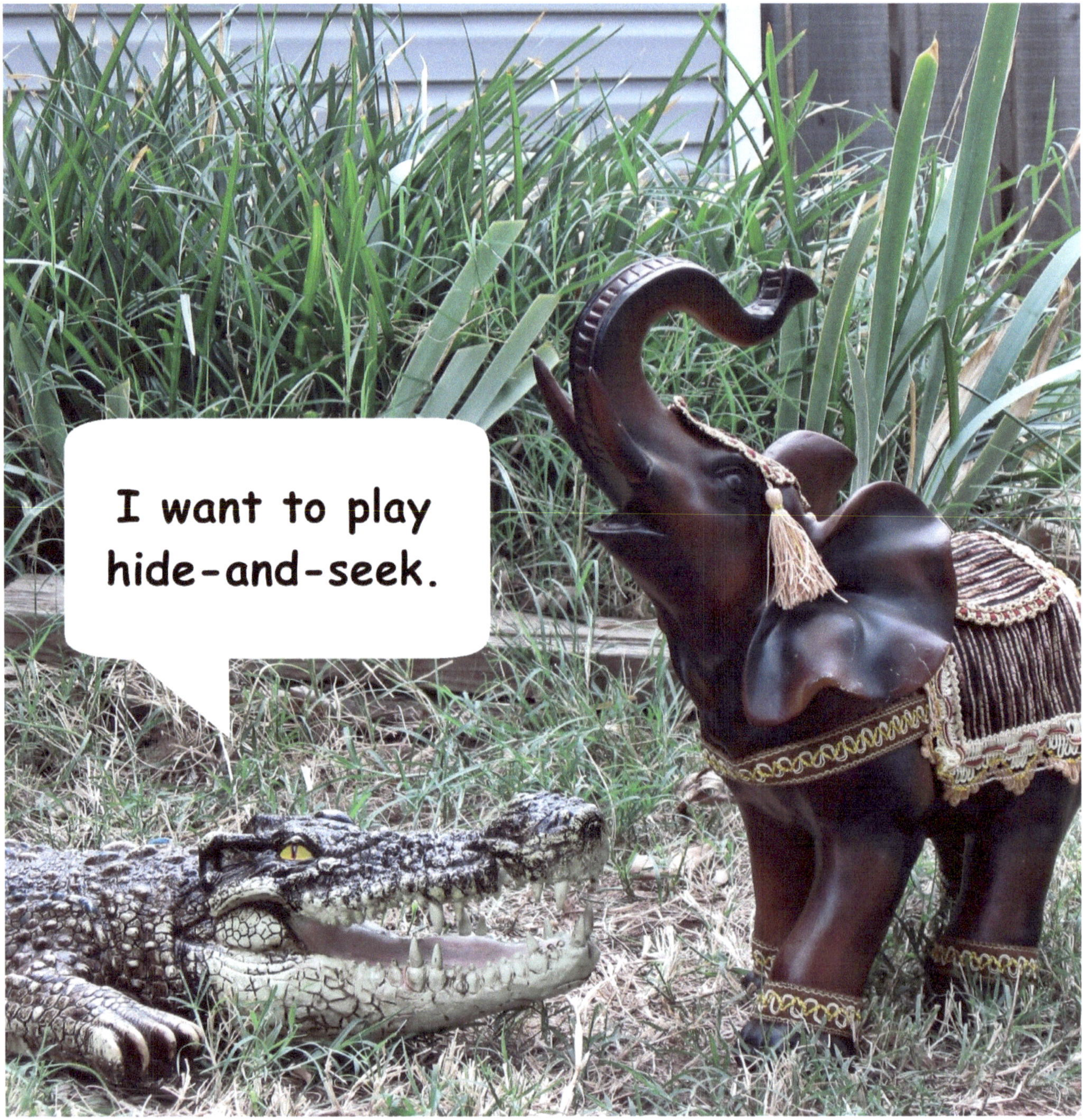
I want to play hide-and-seek.

Ernie Elephant and Cranky Croc will hide. And you can help me find them.

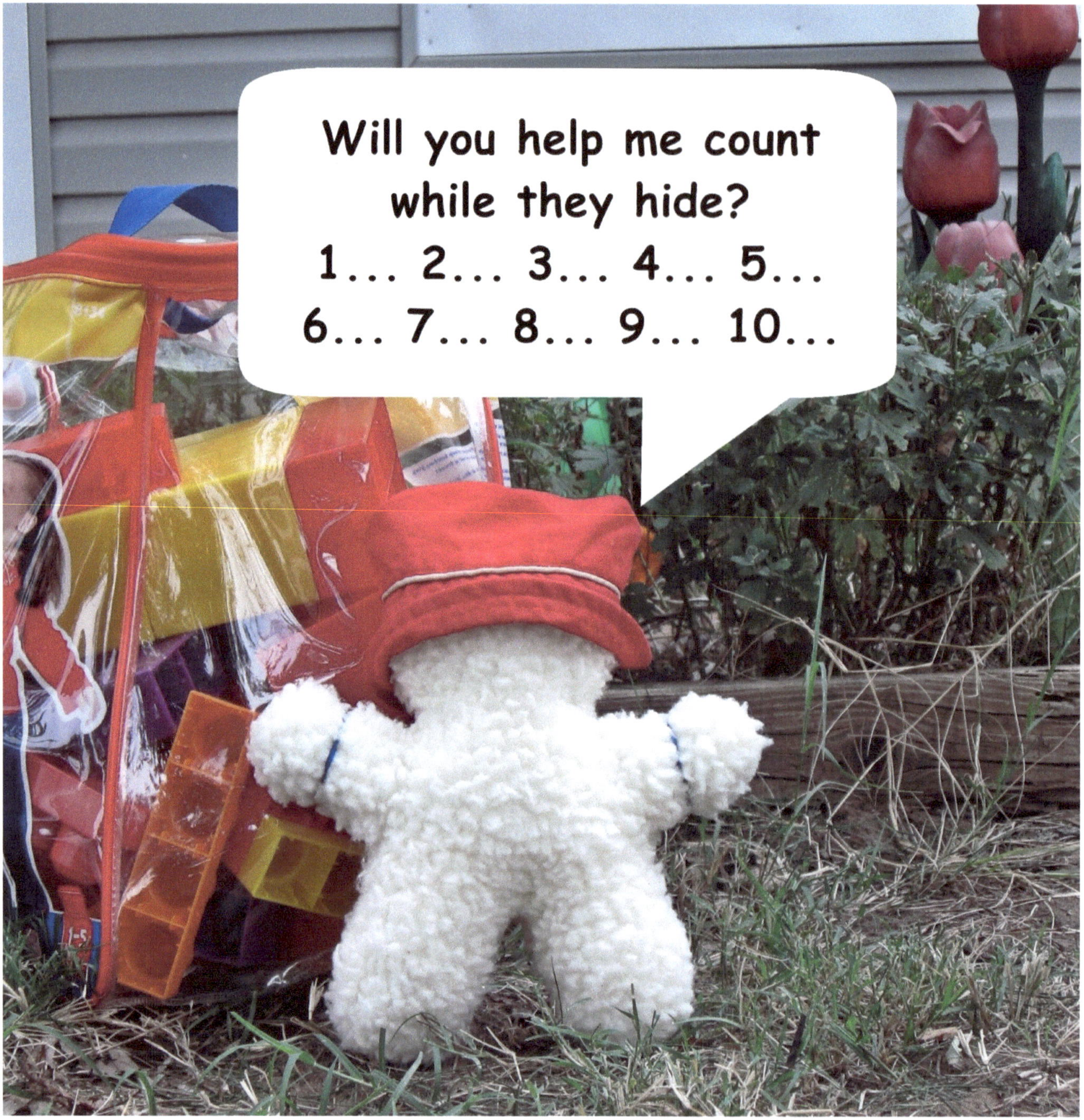
Will you help me count while they hide?
1... 2... 3... 4... 5...
6... 7... 8... 9... 10...

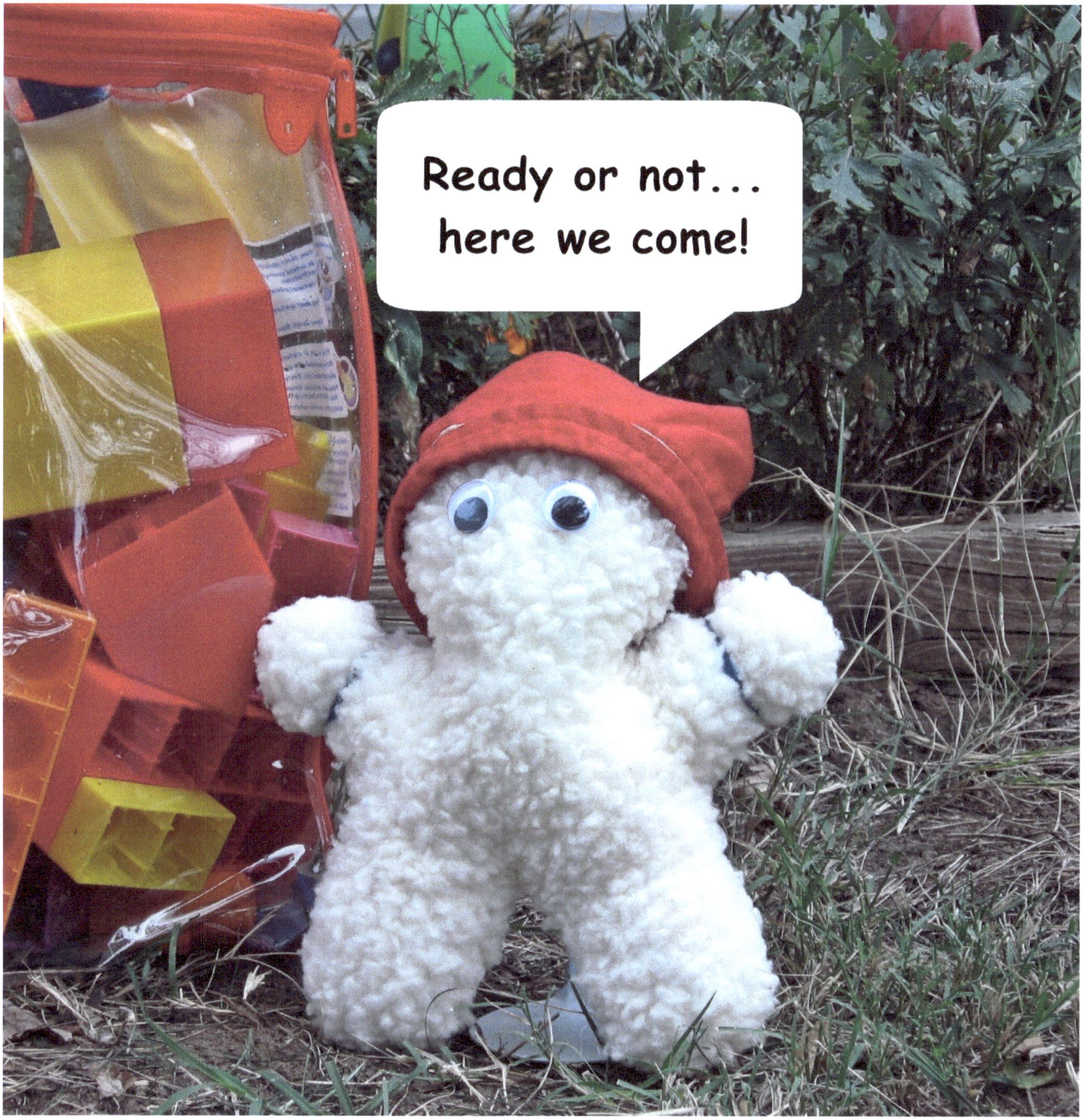
Ready or not...
here we come!

Is Ernie Elephant behind the golf bag?

You are right! Ernie Elephant is not behind the golf bag.

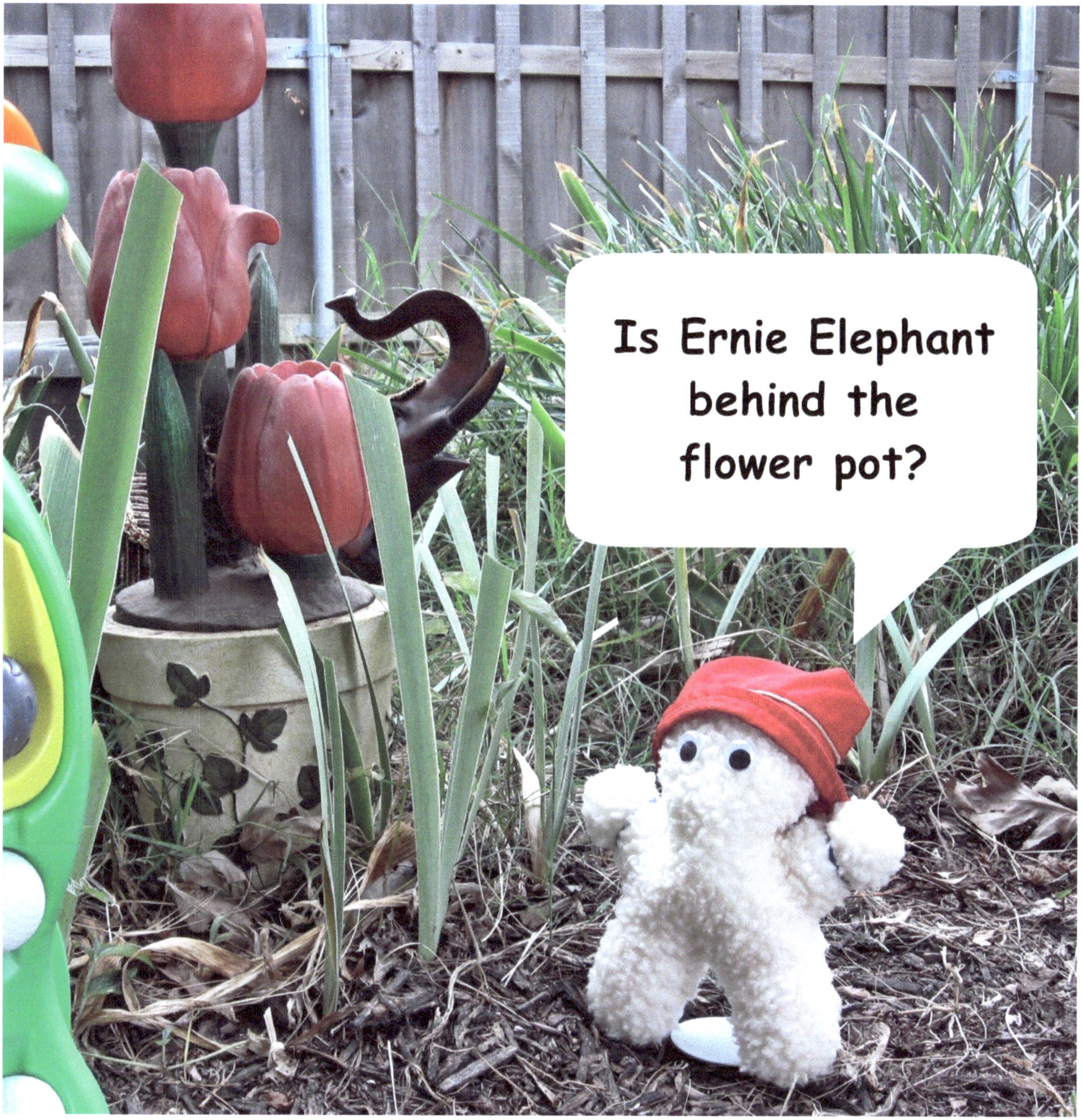
Is Ernie Elephant behind the flower pot?

You are right! Ernie Elephant is behind the flower pot.

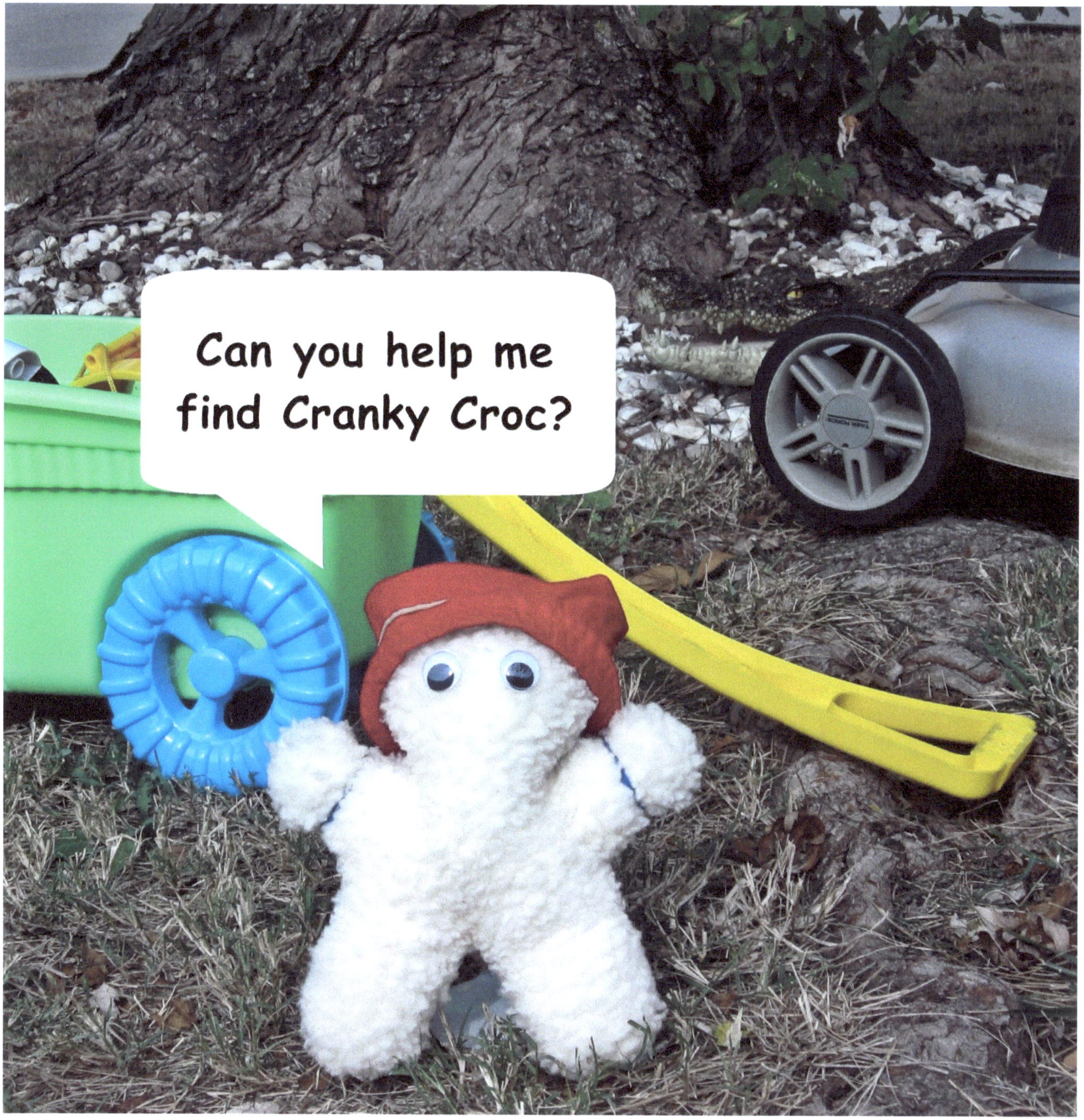
Can you help me find Cranky Croc?

ABOUT THE AUTHOR

Dawn Cawthon Behrens lives in the magical windy kingdom of Stillwater, Oklahoma with her two magnificent cats, Miss Tuxedo and Mister Whiskers, and many fun toys like Benjamin Boo. She spends a lot of time playing with her toys and making up stories about them. She has so much fun with her three grandchildren. She has a B.S. degree in English and an M.A. degree in Theatre, and she has been a teacher, writer, actor, and singer for many years.

The Benjamin Boo children's picture book series also includes the following books:

Benjamin Boo Real Super Hero

Benjamin Boo and the Cranky Crocodile

www.ingramcontent.com/pod-product-compliance
Lightning Source LLC
Chambersburg PA
CBHW041223040426
42443CB00002B/68